MY NEW PET

MY PET PARAKEET

BY NANCY GREENWOOD

Gareth Stevens PUBLISHING

Please visit our website, www.garethstevens.com. For a free color catalog of all our high-quality books, call toll free 1-800-542-2595 or fax 1-877-542-2596.

Portions of this work were originally authored by Cecelia H. Brannon and published as *Pet Parakeets.* All new material this edition authored by Nancy Greenwood.

Library of Congress Cataloging-in-Publication Data
Names: Greenwood, Nancy, author.
Title: My pet parakeet / Nancy Greenwood.
Description: New York : Gareth Stevens Publishing, [2023] | Series: My new pet | Includes index.
Identifiers: LCCN 2022000009 (print) | LCCN 2022000010 (ebook) | ISBN 9781538281086 (set) | ISBN 9781538281093 (library binding) | ISBN 9781538281079 (paperback) | ISBN 9781538281109 (ebook)
Subjects: LCSH: Budgerigar–Juvenile literature.
Classification: LCC SF473.B8 G74 2023 (print) | LCC SF473.B8 (ebook) | DDC 636.6/864–dc23/eng/20220111
LC record available at https://lccn.loc.gov/2022000009
LC ebook record available at https://lccn.loc.gov/2022000010

Published in 2023 by
Gareth Stevens Publishing
29 East 21st Street
New York, NY 10010

Designer: Andrea Davison-Bartolotta
Editor: Kristen Nelson

Photo credits: Cover, p.1 Stasiuk/Shutterstock.com; series art (interior backgrounds) Magnia/Shutterstock.com; p. 5 Aleksandra Moiseeva/Shutterstock.com; p. 7 Soffi/Shutterstock.com; p. 9 Andrew Angelov/Shutterstock.com; p. 11 MYBROS/Shutterstock.com; p. 13 Kolotygin Igor/Shutterstock.com; p. 15 VitCOM Photo/Shutterstock.com; p. 17 C.Ashby/Shutterstock.com; p. 19 BestPhotoStudio/Shutterstock.com; p. 21 Zurijeta/Shutterstock.com.

Printed in the United States of America

CPSIA compliance information: Batch #CSGS23: For further information contact Gareth Stevens, New York, New York at 1-800-542-2595.

CONTENTS

Boldface words appear in the glossary.

Great Pet

Parakeets are **popular** pets! These birds are one of the smallest kinds of bird in the parrot family. They are **native** to Australia. Sometimes parakeets are called budgies. They are **gentle** and friendly. That's why people like them so much!

Colorful Bird

A parakeet has a long tail, a sharp beak, and wings. Parakeets are bright and colorful. They can be green, yellow, blue, or a mix of these and other colors.

Pet Parakeet Life

Parakeets are known for being easy to care for. But, it's still a big **responsibility** to own a bird. Pet parakeets are kept in cages. Be sure the cage is big enough! The cage should be cleaned at least every week.

Your pet parakeet will spend much of its time in its cage on a perch. A perch is a long bar on which the bird can stand and rest. You may need to put a special light next to the cage too.

It's best for pet parakeets to eat food made just for them. Then, you can also give them fresh vegetables, fruit, and seeds sometimes. Parakeets need fresh water too. Water in a parakeet's cage should be changed every day.

Taking Care

Parakeets take baths to stay clean! They need other **grooming** too. Parakeets need their nails trimmed, but this should be done by someone who is trained. Your pet parakeet also may have their wings clipped. Ask your **vet** if that's needed.

Parakeets have their wings clipped so that they don't fly away or hurt themselves. Still, you must let your parakeet out of its cage every now and then. This is how it exercises. Don't leave a window open though!

So Smart!

Parakeets are very smart. They can sing and whistle. They like to play with toys. Parakeets can learn tricks. You can teach a parakeet to sit on your finger. You may be able to teach it to **mimic** some words!

Friend for Life

Getting a pet often means caring for them for their whole life. Pet parakeets can live as long as 12 years. If you take good care of your parakeet, it will be your friend for a long time!

GLOSSARY

gentle: Having a quiet nature.

grooming: The process of cleaning the fur, skin, or feathers.

mimic: To copy.

native: Born in a place.

popular: Liked by many people.

responsibility: Something a person is in charge of.

vet: A doctor who is trained to treat animals. Vet is short for veterinarian.

FOR MORE INFORMATION

BOOKS

Abbott, Simon. *100 Questions About Birds: And All the Answers Too!*. White Plains, NY: Peter Pauper Press, Inc., 2022.

Bankston, John. *Caring for My New Parakeet*. Hallandale, FL: Mitchell Lane Publishing, 2021.

WEBSITES

Key Facts You Need to Know About Pet Birds
kidspetclub.com/basic-facts-you-need-to-know-about-pet-birds/
Should you get a bird? This website can help you learn more and decide.

Parakeet Facts
www.softschools.com/facts/animals/parakeet_facts/1274/
Check out lots of fun facts about parakeets here.

INDEX